The Air Bridge Between Berlin & Me

The Air Bridge Between Berlin & Me

Gemütlichkeit OR Terroristador!

Lance Carden

FOREWORD BY
Marie Laure

RESOURCE *Publications* • Eugene, Oregon

THE AIR BRIDGE BETWEEN BERLIN AND ME
Gemütlichkeit OR Terroristador!

Resource Publications
An Imprint of Wipf and Stock Publishers
199 W. 8th Ave., Suite 3
Eugene, OR 97401

www.wipfandstock.com

PAPERBACK ISBN: 979-8-3852-2953-6
HARDCOVER ISBN: 979-8-3852-2954-3
EBOOK ISBN: 979-8-3852-2955-0

VERSION NUMBER 11/01/24

This book is dedicated to Minno, my grandmother, who was so full of *Gemütlichkeit*.

I grew up in Oklahoma in the so-called United States. Nonetheless, it's sometimes said: "There are East Coast states and West Coast states, Gulf Coast states and Great Lakes states—and all the others are somewhere *in between.*"

Contents

Foreword

BY MARIE LAURE

THE AUTHOR, LANCE CARDEN, has wanted to connect the dots of this story for more than 60 years! To this end, his book is not a legacy memoir; it is one person's mission shared with us at critical junctures in both German and American history.

It opens with a bit of trivia about "Berlin Air," but soon educates us about a major effort undertaken by the United States and England against the Communists in East Berlin in 1948-49. East Germans and Russians were doing all they could to starve out West Berliners and coerce them to join the Communists in East Berlin. We learn how the Berlin Airlift then supplied food and fuel to American troops and to *2 million West Berliners* following World War II. The Airlift lasted more than a year and is described in vivid detail with help from a 75th anniversary Airlift exhibition during the author's third trip to Berlin in 2023.

Carden began life in earnest at age nineteen, when he unexpectedly received $500, more than enough to get him aboard a student ship to Europe. His sole purpose was to conquer the German language, which had so far defeated him at the University of Oklahoma. When he first smells the sea air as the little ship pulls away from the dock, he realizes there is no way to turn back! A pattern of his whole story is set here, reinforced with the refrain: *"I'm getting ahead of myself."* He intricately weaves together stories he wrote on his first trip to Germany with stories of his days as an Air Force officer working in Berlin. Then ties the final knot when as an octogenarian he revisits Berlin as a seasoned, professional writer.

The book meanders from coming of age to finally returning to his beloved Berlin in 2023 with his daughter, who was born in the city. The return is not only to revisit old places but to finish writing what he began decades ago. In some charmingly dated vignettes, he hides himself in full view in the guise of an unpolished, untraveled, unassuming student named Arthur. There is a bit of Arthur in all of us, and we squirm with embarrassment as he awkwardly encounters another culture so different and so far from where he has come.

The middle story focuses on his years as an Air Force officer in West Berlin, connecting us to a time that seems long ago, but also eerily at hand. During three years as a lieutenant or captain with a high-level security clearance, he's told to stay out of East Berlin, or even riding a subway that goes through so-called "ghost stations" in East Berlin. The people he commands spend their working hours listening and watching Russian, Polish, and German military airplanes flying in and around Berlin.

All told, the tapestry of any life is one of wisdom born of pain, joy, and change. This story may be unique in its span of years from the 1960s to the 2020s, when even our fragile democracy seems about to change. Reader beware!

Marie Laure is the author of three books: Tuscan Retreat *(2013),* Chances Are . . . *(2016),* Return from Exile *(2021).*

Acknowledgments

First, I want to say how many ways my wife, Charlene Vincent, helped me write and finish this book. She not only encouraged me, she talked about it day by day. She edited the manuscript and suggested corrections. In 2023, she organized our trip to England, the Netherlands, and Germany. She went with me and took many of the photographs (all others are by the author). A neighbor of ours, Kathy Koberstein, read many versions of the book and made very helpful suggestions. My grandson, Henry Siegl, helped by drawing two illustrations. A friend, David Salisbury, read the manuscript, made very clever suggestions, and then helped me with the photos. Katherine Frazier and Kathleen Trued read a print of the book and corrected a number of mistakes. My daughter, Laura Carden, came to visit us in Berlin and helped us find our way about the city. My special thanks to all of them.

PART I

Gemütlichkeit

1

The Air Bridge

WHEN I WAS IN Berlin in the 1960s, souvenir shops sold cans of *Berliner Luft*, which translates to "Berlin Air." And that was all it was—it was *only air*! The city's breath is nothing special, but I believe those little cans appeared after what is called the *Luftbrücke*, or Air Bridge. In English, we call it the Airlift, which saved millions of West Berliners from starving or joining the Communists in East Germany after World War II.

Some historians say the Berlin Airlift was the first battle of the Cold War. Known as Operation Plainfare by the British and Operation Vittles by the Americans, the Airlift helped make *Berliner Luft* a popular souvenir.

After the war, Germany was split down the middle: West Germany on one side, East Germany on the other. That left Berlin, the former capital, nearly a hundred miles east of the border between West and East Germany. The city was divided into four sectors: British, French, Russian, and American.

In 1948, as tensions grew between the Western sectors and the Russian sector, the Russians tried to get the upper hand. They blockaded all waters, roads, and rail tracks that went through East Germany to reach Berlin. That meant the only way to feed and fuel the allied troops in West Berlin, plus some *two million* West Berliners, was through the air.

The Russians were confident this could not be done—and without food and fuel, West Berliners would be forced to become part of East Germany. It was an act of terror, and fortunately it misfired. For more than a year, British and American military planes fed and fueled half of one of Europe's largest cities *through the air!*

I'm going to say more about the Airlift, because without it I might never have been in Berlin, might never have met my first wife, might never have had a child, and might never have worked at Tempelhof, an airport so important to the Airlift.

How did I, a teenager from Oklahoma, come to be in Germany? Well, it all goes back to my grandmother, whose nickname was Minno. She lived in a small house with me, my parents, and my three siblings. Minno was born of German immigrants, and she spoke German before she learned English. She liked to tell us about her younger years in Texas, where her family and other German immigrants were part of a social club. They would go to the club house after church on Sunday to celebrate the week with German food and wine or beer.

But that came to a halt when World War I began; the club ceased to be and her family stopped speaking German, at least in public. I never heard Minno speak anything but English.

Her real name was Elizabeth Burch; as a result, I was named Lance Burch Carden. She was a second mother to each of us four children. There was something regal about her calm, determined attitude. My younger brother, David, often said she was the wisest woman he ever met. Minno knew something—not about the world, but about herself—something I wanted for *myself.*

Minno loved working in our garden and playing cards with all us kids. She and my mother liked to go to the Wichita Mountains Wildlife Refuge, twenty minutes from where we lived. They liked to see the buffalo and many other needy creatures. This refuge was the first national attempt to keep buffalo from going extinct. Our family went there nearly every week, but we didn't think of it as a refuge for buffalo or other animals. We thought it was a refuge for folks like us who wanted to explore the creeks, the mountains, the deer, the turtles, and then to adore *our refuge*, as we certainly did!

My gentle grandmother and her German heritage impelled me to take a German-language class as a freshman at the University of Oklahoma. When I went home on weekends, Minno and I sometimes sat in our back yard and drank small glasses of Manischewitz wine, which was too sweet for me, but made me feel almost adult—for only adults could buy alcohol. This we did in secret, because alcohol was usually forbidden in our home. Nonetheless, in the summer, my father would sometimes drink a beer—not in our house, but in our back yard—after he came home from work. He was only allowed to put one can of beer in the very back of our "icebox" (refrigerator), for we children were not to be exposed to alcohol.

After I had taken three semesters of German, I was so frustrated with my progress that I left the university in January, went back home, and worked in a hotel for about seven months, saving what little I earned to pay for a year of study in West Germany. In the 1960s, study abroad was very unusual, especially for undergraduates. When I realized in early August that I could not earn enough to go to Germany that year, I started preparing for another semester at the university. But then, out of the blue, a home-town foundation suddenly gave me a five-hundred-dollar grant, which seemed enormous to me. I had asked for this some months before, but had forgotten all about it. As a result, I found myself caught up *in between*: I wanted to go back to the university, but I could not turn down five hundred bucks! Without accepting that grant, my year in Germany would have been impossible—and my life would have been completely different.

I knew this for sure when I stood on the windy deck of a Holland America ship about to sail from New York to Rotterdam. The deck was full of students like me, for this was the cheapest way to go to Europe. As the ship moved away, I saw a crowd waving us their good-byes. This left me teary-eyed, because I knew there was no way to turn back. As an Oklahoman, I had never seen an ocean or a sea, much less been on top of one in a little ship—a *very little* ship, which took about ten days to get us to Rotterdam.

Soon after I shed tears, I thought I heard five or six people speaking German. So, I stepped close to them to see if I could understand what they were saying. Suddenly, one of them turned to me and said in English:

"Can we help you?"

Knowing I had been found out, I responded:

"I just wanted to see if I could understand your German."

To which my interlocutor replied:

"No, we *cannot* help you; we are speaking Dutch."

On our long voyage to Rotterdam, I got to know one of those Dutch students. One day, as I was sitting with her, I saw a German student I had also met, and asked her if she would like to meet him.

"No, she said, "he looks too German for me; I do not want to meet him." Then she told me some of the things German soldiers had done while they occupied the Netherlands for five long years during WWII.

This book is an attempt to make art out of some history and family lore. It's not a novel or novella, not a history or a travelogue, not a memoir, nor just a few short stories that hang together with a few stanzas of poetry. It is all that mixed together like scrambled eggs!

There are three intertwined stories: One is about me in Germany as a student in 1961-62. Then, from '65 to '68, I am an Air Force officer in Berlin. It's what happened to me when I was too young to know that I was getting ahead of myself—that I should have known more about myself and the much, much wider world before going out there. Do I regret it? No, I certainly do not. But even then, I knew it could be very lonely out in the wide, wide world. The third story is about my return to Berlin in 2023, more than five decades later. Why was I returning? Because we in America were beginning to see what Germans saw nearly a century ago: The possibility that one man could rule our whole country with intimidation, fear, and lots of violence.

I was still nineteen when I first went to Germany, and still in my twenties in 1968, when I left the Air Force and the city of Berlin to come back to the United States. Now, in 2023, I have returned as a poet, a former journalist, and an octogenarian who hopes to tell his little stories of being a student in Germany. Even as an undergrad, I knew I wanted to be a writer. So, while I was in Germany decades ago, I wrote some stories about my experiences there. I hope you will read them as flashbacks, as though you are watching a movie in which I disguise myself as someone named Arthur.

2

Berlin, Oct. 1, 1961 (late afternoon)

ARTHUR HAS PASSED AN hour on *Kurfürstendamm*, a street (or *Strasse*) with expensive shops. When he reaches Kaiser Wilhelm Memorial Church, he notices there are actually two buildings: One is a bombed-out, 19th-century edifice; the other is glassy and modern. A sign says the older one stands as a monument to the horrible reality of war.

When Arthur walks into the new building, he does so with a sigh of relief. Leaving Berlin's crowded sidewalks and traffic arteries is like entering the peaceful eye of a storm. When he emerges from the church, his ears are not only refilled with the noise of the city but with the sound of rain, for which he has no umbrella. He is tired of sightseeing, and it's too early for dinner, so Arthur steps quickly across a busy street into a coffee bar.

The pungent smell of coffee seems trapped inside by the rain. At one counter, coffee beans are ground, packaged, and sold by the gram or kilo. At another counter, freshly brewed coffee is served by a grey-haired woman in white, who places two white cubes of sugar on a saucer and a dash of cream in a cup before pouring the coffee and handing the steaming beverage to customer after customer. That done, she rings up twenty *pfennigs* on the register and automatically reaches for the next saucer. There are no seats; customers stand, resting cups and saucers on small circular tables, all of them occupied by at least one person.

As Arthur is paying for his coffee, he notices a young woman with short black hair looking back at him. So, approaching her, he asks in German if he might share her table. She replies with a nod of her head. Her back is to the street, and she is drawing luxuriously on a filtered cigarette, its tip frosted pink with lipstick. Long bangs hang almost to her eyebrows, concealing her forehead. Her cup is empty, so Arthur asks in German if she would like more coffee.

"*Ja, bitte*" (Yes, please), she replies.

Relieved, Arthur walks away with her empty cup, sets it on a table near the counter, gets in line behind two tall youths in work uniforms, places another twenty *pfennigs* in a glass tray, and takes a fresh cup of coffee from the woman in white.

On his return, he notices the woman across from him is wearing a green jersey under an opened suede coat, which falls loosely from her shoulders. When he pushes her cup across the table, she lights another cigarette and smiles her thanks with an exhale of smoke. Trying with difficulty to start a conversation in German, Arthur says something about the rain.

"Oh, this?" she replies, pointing back to the street. "Yes, it's disgraceful this weather. On the Mediterranean, they're still swimming."

"Yes, yes," he agrees, delighted with her response, trying to remember to think in German, and wondering how he might reply.

"Are you American?" she asks, dissolving his tangled thought.

"Yes, that's right. I'm in Berlin since yesterday." Smiling across the table, he asks: "Are you from Berlin?"

"No. I'm from Magdeburg."

"From where?"

"From the East." Then the question, which at nineteen he's never been asked: "Are you a soldier?"

"No."

"How long have you been in Germany?"

"Two weeks."

"You speak German well for just two weeks."

"I study German in America . . . at a university."

"You're a student?"

"Yes."

"I'm still a school girl," she replies, blinking her eyes coquettishly. He smiles back, wondering about her exact age, but not really caring.

"My name's Arthur. What's yours?"

"Karin."

"Would you like to show me a bit of Berlin?"

"What would you like to see?" she asks, tilting her head to one side with a grin full of straight, white teeth. He's not sure if she's feigning interest or mocking him. Nonetheless, he gives a short rundown of sights he's seen over the past two days, including a long bus tour of West Berlin and trying out two subway systems, one of them running through East Berlin, where there are no stops. Finally, he confesses he has only one more day in Berlin before going to the Goethe Institute, a language school in Bad Aibling, West Germany.

"I've already seen the things I think I ought to see, but I haven't met any *people*. I want to know what people are like here, what they're thinking."

This statement is to clarify his situation, to let her know that he's not an ordinary tourist. Karin gives him no response. Stubbing out her cigarette, only half-finished, she stares dubiously across the table before asking:

"Would you like to go shopping?"

"For what?"

"Nothing in particular . . . just *looking*. I got a pension today, so I can afford to buy something. It's more fun if you're with someone."

"Yes, I'd like to, very much."

Without any more words, Karin picks up her purse from under the table, and Arthur follows her out the door, where the drizzle has stopped. Her jacket falls well below her short skirt. Her walk is leisurely, self-conscious, feminine.

"Where are we going?"

"To *Ka De We*."

"What's that?"

"You'll see."

On the way, she says *Ka De We* stands for *Kaufhaus des Westens* (Store of the West), one of the largest department stores in Germany. At the entrance, she buys two *Salzstangen* from a one-armed man with a box strapped around his shoulders; then she hands Arthur one of the long, thin bread sticks, crusty and heavily salted.

Inside *Ka De We*, the rich visual display surprises Arthur, who has seen nothing like this in Oklahoma. Above long counters supporting thick rolls of satins, velvets, linens, and worsted fabrics, are colorful displays of bright synthetic fibers and patterned cottons. Some drape down from tall slender mannequins. He has only a moment to enjoy the spectacle, as Karin leads him into the crush of shoppers stroking, admiring, and evaluating a seemingly limitless supply of merchandise.

They cannot see some of the discount tables; which are screened from their vision by eager customers. Karin stops at one less-crowded display, pulling the corner of a roll of chiffon like a veil across her elfin face, blinking her eyes at him, and giggling. From time to time, she stops to take a bite of her *Salzstange* and to glance back at Arthur, pushing his way courteously but awkwardly through clusters of matronly housewives.

After the Materials Department, comes Cosmetics, then Soaps and Pharmaceuticals. Karin holds out a perfume bottle for him to smell, and then a box of scented soap. Mounting a staircase to the second floor, Arthur watches a middle-aged man dig through a bin of black and brown wallets, as though searching for hidden treasure.

As they work their way slowly through the Musical Records section, Karin points out various albums she wants to buy as soon as she has a turntable. She is also saving for a guitar. Later, she shows him a few other things she intends to buy, as well as some Danish furniture for an apartment of her own.

"What sort of pension do you receive?" asks Arthur, as they leave Furniture and enter Gardening.

"I get an orphan's pension from the city."

"I see . . ."

"Ah, the toys!" she cries, pulling him down a side aisle. After they have browsed their way through numerous stuffed animals, games, and mechanical toys, Arthur sees a promotion of Super Balls.

"Do you know about Super Balls?" he asks, taking one from the basket.

"No, I don't think so."

"You do it like this," he says, stepping away from her and bouncing the ball from one hand to the other. Arthur then bounces it to Karin, who squeals at the speed of the small red ball, which bounces through her outstretched hands and careens off her shoulder. The ball is all the way back to Arthur before she can catch up with it.

"There's something very American about a Super Ball," she says, looking up at him. Arthur heads to the cashier's desk, and when he returns, he hands her the ball in a brown paper bag.

"It's yours," he says, noting a sudden sparkle in her eyes.

"Danke schön, Arthur!" (Thank you, Arthur!)

"Would you like to have dinner with me?" he asks, as they make their way back downstairs.

"I can't. My aunt expects me in thirty minutes."

Sensing his disappointment, she adds: "But I would really like to." And she takes his arm as they continue down the stairs and emerge from *Ka De We*. The sidewalk is still wet, but the sky is clear.

"Where do you live?" he asks.

"In Spandau."

"How do you get home?"

"On the bus."

"Where do you catch it?"

"Back there," she says, pointing. "On the other side of the church; I must hurry, or my aunt will be angry."

Noticing a pedestrian light is turning green, Arthur grabs her hand and begins to run.

"Let's go!"

He pulls her into a sudden effort to make the light, but as they reach an island in the middle of the street, the green light turns to amber. Karin tries to stop, but Arthur pulls her on across two traffic lanes, as the amber switches to red. Karin stumbles at the curb, dropping her purse and the paper bag with the Super Ball. After he helps her regain her balance, Arthur chases the bouncing bag across the wet sidewalk toward the concrete base of a shoe store. An old man, dressed in a bulky loden coat, takes a dark cigar from his mouth and shakes it at them defiantly:

"*Politzei!*" he warns, although there are no policemen in the vicinity. An elderly couple, walking past them with a Doberman on a short leash, cast their own disparaging glances. The couple tries to pass aloofly by, but their dog has spied a bouncing paper bag, hopping like a rabbit along the sidewalk. With a loud bark, the Doberman hits the end of his leash, aided by a sharp tug from his mistress. Then she, too, sees the bouncing bag, and grabbing her companion's arm, she says: "*Kuck, Heinrich!*" (Look, Heinrich!).

The dog wants to play, but his owners do not; to Arthur, he's a child and they are adults. The woman points; the old man fishes bifocals out of his overcoat; Karin recovers her purse; the bouncing bag reaches the base of a store front and rebounds toward Arthur. One additional bounce, and he retrieves it with the ease of a shortstop.

As Arthur looks around, the traffic lights change, and cars come to a halt. Knowing he's the center of attention, Arthur smiles, wraps the wet bag tightly about the ball, and bounces both bag and ball off the sidewalk high up into the air, defying laws of gravity and dignity. He lets the bag bounce once more above his head, then hauls it in.

The old man, leaning on a black umbrella, holds tightly to one corner of his bifocals. The other man

and his wife move on, dragging the barking Doberman behind. Then the lights change and vehicles move
again. Karin, laughing hysterically, grabs the bag from
Arthur, bounces it off a building, catches the rebound,
and bounces it back to him. The two of them are
moving up the busy thoroughfare, from time to time
bouncing a magical paper bag off the sidewalk and
through the air from one to the other to the aston-
ishment of passersby. Past the bombed-out Memorial
Church, in both its bombed-out and modern incarna-
tions, and toward the bus stop near *Bahnhof Zoo*.

When they get to the bus stop, Karin tells Arthur he
should go to the Old Eden Saloon, which is very close
by. He says he will and then invites her to meet him
there at 9 p.m.

"I don't know if I can. But if my aunt allows, I will meet
you there. Anyway, you *must* go. Many young people
go there, many tourists, and Americans."

"Do you know many Americans?" he asks.

"No."

There is a pause as they wait for the bus. She is looking
down the street as if to see whether the bus is coming.
But then she asks him a peculiar question:

"Do you believe in a just war?"

"What do you mean, 'a just war'?"

"I mean has there ever been a war worth fighting?"

"Oh . . . of course," he says, struggling with his German.
"The American Revolution was fought for freedom.
That's worth it, don't you think?"

"No. I don't believe war is ever right. That's why I don't
know any Americans. In Berlin, most of them are soldiers. This is an *occupied* city, you know!"

16

"Is that why you don't believe in war, because Germany lost the last two?"

"No! Not because we lost, but because I lost a father who thought it was a 'just war.'"

"But, if Germany had won, and your father were a kind of hero, then maybe you'd feel different."

"I hope not."

Then comes the bus, and it's all over. She shakes his hand awkwardly, smiles, and climbs aboard as he shouts a hopeful goodbye and hears her brief reply:

"My father really is a hero!"

Then she's out of sight, and the door closes—without a kiss, a phone number, or *even an address!*

3

Danke Schön!
(Thank You Very Much!)

To me, that pensioned orphan named Karin, whom I was so happy to meet (and disappointed not to re-meet) was like many young Berliners. They had lost their childhood to the Nazis and a brutal war. It would take many Super Balls to give them back what they now lacked.

Several decades ago, a woodcut print fell into my hands: I'm going to describe the people in this picture because it says more than my words can. As I view it, these are two women, possibly sisters or a mother and child, living without a father or husband, who didn't return from the war. One of them is sitting at a table, staring ahead as though there is no tomorrow or any expectations. Another woman is looking at her with the most anguished eyes as she pours some coffee into her empty cup. It is clear how closely they are bonded, the one to the other. They can't go back and don't know how to go forward, except to care for one another.

Rudolf Weissauer made this print in 1950. What also greatly interests me is a three-inch plaque nailed to the bottom of the wooden frame. It says: *Dankspende des Deutschen Volkes 1951* (Thanksgiving from the German People 1951).

German President Theodor Heuss appealed to the German public to support this so-called Thanksgiving in a radio address that year. Translated into English, he said: "This is not a political affair; it is primarily a human one. Gratefulness exalts a nation, because it is the attitude of free men." Many of the funds donated were between 2 and 5 marks, when 4 marks was about a dollar. But the donations added up to 1.5 million marks! With these funds, the non-profit gave some German artists a little income by purchasing their works and then giving them to foreign donors as a gesture of thanks, or *Danke schön!* President Heuss later said: "Based on my experience . . . I can positively say that the desire to thank is a deeply felt and strong one among the German people."[1] An expert jury carefully selected the works to portray a generation of Germans.

Weissauer's woodcut print helps me feel their pain.

Many Germans were able to survive after the war, especially the winter of '46-'47, because of goods and money donated by foreigners. None of this was part of the Marshall Plan, the U.S. Economic Recovery Act of 1948. So, in the early 1950s, *Dankspende des Deutschen Volkes* was giving ordinary Germans a chance to display some special thanks.

---

1. The quotes from President Heuss are taken from an Information Bulletin, University of Wisconsin-Madison Libraries, March 1952.

How did I come to have this piece of expressionist art? For some decades, beginning in 1971, I was a journalist at *The Christian Science Monitor* newspaper. Weissauer's print was probably given to the Christian Science Church as part of an estate. Monetarily speaking, the framed print is not worth much, so the church decided it could be auctioned off to any employee who made the highest bid. I think I bought this framed print for about ninety dollars.

I wanted it because I thought I knew what *Dankspende des Deutschen Volkes* means: That this print is an historical piece of art, showing the personal aftermath of what we call WWII. It captured my heart, because I knew there were so many Germans like the couple in this print.

4

Berlin, Oct. 1, 1961 (evening)

ARTHUR IS SITTING UNDER a crude balcony against the back wall of Old Eden's front bar. He's watching the entrance, hoping to see Karin and wondering if she will come. Outside, the saloon occupies one corner of an otherwise solid rectangle of tenements near this end of *Kurfürstendamm*. Inside, it looks old and wasted, full of smoke and the smell of beer. The room is crowded, making his vigil difficult. A wooden ladder partially obscures his view. A couple about his own age occupy the next table. Arthur thinks they're speaking French, but a recorded Brandenburg Concerto is so loud he cannot be sure.

Above the bar to Arthur's left are three projectors and some sort of rope and pulley by which drinks are passed to a small satellite bar on the other side of the room. One projector is beaming a Charlie Chaplin movie against the wall above the bar. There are more men than women; most of them wearing sweaters. Heavy coats can be left with a hat-check girl off the entrance. It's 9:20 p.m.

Arthur has never seen anything like the Old Eden Saloon. He knows Berlin's reputation for exotic night life, but he did not expect something as cool as this.

"Thank goodness I was able to meet Karin!" he thinks.

Old Eden Saloon circa 1965
Photo by Mirrorpix

When the concerto ends, one of the projectors flashes a series of slides onto the wall above the entrance. Each slide lasts about thirty seconds. The first shows a naked girl with long black hair. Her body is turned away from the camera, as she glances back over her shoulder. In the next slide, a brunette in white tights restrains a greyhound with a leash. Arthur's glass of beer, his second, is half-empty as a new recording begins:

Freight Train

High on another wall is a TV set, where a symphony concert is being performed without sound. The conductor waves hands and arms gracefully, and like chorus girls, members of the violin section move their arms and heads in unison. Then, in silence, the woodwinds do the same, as the recording of *Freight Train* wails on:

One of the slide projectors throws a sculpture image up high on the wall—a tall, thin, emaciated figure, bare and vulnerable. When someone changes the record, a couple on the other side of Arthur slide back into their chairs. He lights her cigarette, then his, just as Charlie Chaplin is replaced by Buster Keaton on the wall to the right.

A second film, homemade and amateurish, appears on the wall next to Keaton's. It's of a young girl naked to the waist riding a motorcycle, long blond hair flowing behind. First, the camera is behind, then in front of her, as she speeds unsteadily along a country road. Motorcycle bouncing, her breasts bouncing, as the girl without a crash helmet laughs and waves.

Another record begins with the song *Can't Buy Me Love*.

Buster Keaton is operating an old-fashioned filling station out in the desert. A big, brawny competitor builds a new-fangled station on the other side of the highway. He challenges Buster to some baseball practice. Buster starts out pitching. His giant protagonist drives each pitch into the tarpaper structure of Buster's dilapidated station.

Finally, Buster gets wise and says: "My turn to bat," eyeing the new station across the highway. But he swings wildly, continually missing the ball. Every pitch whizzing past him rips more holes in his unsteady shack until it is ready to collapse. One more pitch, and the building teeters, but maintains a precarious balance until Buster, running to retrieve the ball, enters the structure and it caves in on top of him in a cloud of dust. On the TV, the symphony audience silently applauds.

As Arthur finishes his beer, another nude statue appears over the entrance. Arthur thinks it's a Modigliani. He gets up, pushes himself around some tables, and passes under the TV set, stepping into a much smaller room behind the main bar. It's quieter here. Some music spills in from the front room, but it is less crowded and there are no movies or projectors. Straight ahead is a curtained entrance to yet another bar, but Arthur turns left into a narrow passageway to another part of Old Eden.

Arthur has already toured the premises, searching for Karin, hoping she has come in without him seeing her. In this room, no one is standing, and there are still plenty of empty seats. Only expensive bottled beer is sold here, mostly to couples. Some look up at him, then return to whispered conversations. The music is recorded blues, along with some progressive jazz. One wall is lined with blown-up facial studies of Marcel Marceau. Another supports a single expressionist painting of a girl's face.

"There'll be nothing like this in Bad Aibling," Arthur says to himself as he walks past a circular bar, into a passageway that forces him to turn ninety degrees right, then ninety left. Now he enters a large refreshment and game room with only a few customers, some playing *Fussball* (a game of manipulated soccer players). Others are eating *Wurst* (sausage), but none of them is Karin.

As he thinks about Old Eden, he deeply regrets not having Karin's address. "Why didn't I ask her?" Of course, he was expecting to see her again at Old Eden; nonetheless, he should have asked her address!

Next, he enters a tiny room, poorly ventilated, featuring live jazz. Vibes, saxophone, and a piano player in one corner are covered with perspiration and are searching slowly and methodically for a mutually satisfying climax. The remainder of the room is lined with spectators, serious and intent. Still no Karin!

Arthur starts toward the last of the Old Eden rooms. As he enters, he runs into a crowd watching a few couples on a dance floor. Some make no pretense of dancing, but simply embrace their partners. Arthur wanders back to the men's room near the refreshment area. Above one of the urinals, his attention is grabbed by a piece of graffiti with an image and the words "Kilroy was here." Below these words, are two small eyes and where there should be a nose, there's something that looks more like a penis.

Arthur knows Kilroy was a rivet inspector paid by the number of rivets he checked, as recorded in chalk. To avoid having his marks erased, he wrote "Kilroy was here" on the machinery. For reasons Arthur doesn't know, others in the military began tagging places they visited with the same words! Suddenly aware of his irritation over the pervasive presence of Americans—especially GIs—in Germany, Arthur finds himself exclaiming out loud, to no one in particular:

"We Americans are so *goofy!*"

5

My Work at Tempelhof

HERE IS PART OF a letter I sent to my family after my first week back in Berlin in 1965. My mother kept it in a folder of things I wrote or sent to her:

> Dear Mom, Dad, Minna, David, + whoever else might read this,
>
> Please excuse my failure to write. This is no evil sign of depression or sickness, but a reflection of my total immersion in the City this 1st week. Berlin has overwhelmed me. The City is not really beautiful, not really gay, not comfortable, not perfect in any respect, yet Berlin is more cosmopolitan and alive than Vienna and more livable than Paris. It is N.Y. without the hunger and ugliness and violence. More than anything else Berlin is invigorating and healthy.

From 1965 to '68, I could not drive out of Berlin to West Germany, nor could I take a regular train out of the city. Because I had a top-secret security clearance, I had to either fly in or out of Berlin or take a military train to be sure that I wouldn't be kidnapped and interrogated.

At Tempelhof, I had about forty people working under me to listen to what pilots of Russian, East German, or Polish military planes said to their ground controllers—and what ground controllers said to them. We also tracked movements of these planes and tried to know as much as possible what those planes were capable of doing.

My supervisor, a major, was of little help. When he transferred out and another came in, the new one told me it was time for my annual recruitment conversation. When I said I had never had such a conversation, he pulled out some papers and told me what I had reportedly said: That I would not stay in the military unless there was "all-out war." That was probably correct, but I never said so, especially to my supervisor.

There were three other groups of about forty people in my Air Force squadron, so one group or another was working around the clock. Each had an officer, usually a lieutenant or captain, and we worked under another officer, a major. The four of us lower officers were so offended by my first supervisor (by the things he said to us, which I won't repeat, even half a century later) that we all decided to volunteer to go to the war in Vietnam. We did this to suggest to the higher ups how much we regretted working under this supervisor. Unfortunately, I was the only one chosen to go to Vietnam, where I expected to learn some French. (*Can you believe this?*) Fortunately, one of the other officers wanted to make a career of the military, and he asked if I would allow him to tell our commander (a colonel) that he wanted to go to Vietnam much more than I did.

I agreed.

At first, our commander said he could not question orders that came down from above, but when my friend said he would ask his father, one of the leaders of the American Legion, to seek an investigation of why his son could not go to Vietnam, our commander changed his mind and the orders were changed. As a result, I stayed in Berlin for a full three years. When I was leaving the Air Force in 1968, I wrote a letter to a post-graduate school saying that "The most valuable aspect of the four years I spent in the Air Force has been the opportunity to live for three years in Berlin."

In the same letter, I wrote:

> I entered the Air Force because I felt obligated, and I am separating because that obligation has been fulfilled. I had hoped as an officer to be able to influence decisions which would in turn affect those serving under me. In this regard, I was too often disappointed, and the satisfaction I knew at times has been outweighed by the unpleasantries of military discipline and bureaucracy.

Asked by a Berliner what I thought of the Vietnam War, I said I supported it because the United States was such a great place to live. But I don't think I was speaking from the heart. My father was an accountant and eventually the civilian manager of the Post Exchange in Fort Sill, Oklahoma, just outside my home town. A Post Exchange is a place where Americans in the military can buy all kinds of things at low prices. My father had never been in the military, but he was politically conservative. Asked at Oklahoma University if I would sign a petition against the war in Vietnam (a petition which would be published in a newspaper *with all our names*), I said I really wanted to sign it but would not, because my father would be so disappointed.

Ironically, it was at Tempelhof Airport's Post Exchange that I met my wife-to-be. Her father was a Pan American pilot who flew in and out of Berlin. I think at that time Pan Am pilots who flew out of Berlin were paid more than pilots elsewhere. In any case, the mother of my wife-to-be did not like living in Berlin. Before I knew it, her whole family was about to move back to their home in Oakland, California. The day before she was to fly to Oakland, we played a round of golf. Before we were finished, I had proposed and she had accepted. Soon after, we were married in Oakland. Of course, we were very young and our marriage did not last, but that is the story of my life.

6

Bad Aibling, Nov. 22, 1961

INCREASINGLY UNCOMFORTABLE UNDER THE eiderdown, Arthur swings his legs over the side of the bed,
pulls off his underwear, and begins to wash at the sink.
He has three pairs of socks, but just two pieces of un-
derpants and just two undershirts, which means he
washes something each time he bathes. There's no hot
water, so he doesn't bathe very often.

Twenty minutes later, Arthur is warming himself in a
restaurant at the Linnter, a hotel in Bad Aibling, a small
town south of Munich. Double doors keep the room
warm and cozy. The hotel isn't cheap, but the price of coffee is. Plus, Arthur can spend hours reading a variety of
German newspapers provided for hotel guests.

Arthur's order is taken by a waitress with golden hair,
who greets him in impeccable Bavarian style:

"*Grüss Gott.*" (May God greet you.)

"*Grüss Gott, Fräulein,*" he replies.

He likes this waitress. She does not seem shy like most young women in the village. She has a beautiful complexion and infectious smile, although her pink cheeks seem to suggest a certain embarrassment.

"Was wünsche der Herr?" (What would the gentleman like?)

"Kaffee, bitte" (Coffee, please).

She is back quickly with silver coffee service and a porcelain cup and saucer. In the meantime, Arthur has picked up an issue of *Süddeutsche Zeitung* (*South German Newspaper*) from a rack of newspapers. But for some reason he does not take out his Langenscheidt Pocket Dictionary, and doesn't begin the ritual of translation. Instead, he succumbs to a reflective train of thought that began under the eiderdown.

He looks at the steaming coffee, at the frosted double-glazing of the hotel windows, and at the freshly printed newspaper, strapped between wooden slats and suspended over arms of a chair. In the tasteful Lintner dining room, he senses he might be experiencing something like *Gemütlichkeit*.

The term *Gemütlichkeit* is Arthur's favorite German word. The first two syllables sound like "gun mute" without the "n." So, if one pronounces it as *Gu-mute-lich-keit* (with the accent on "mute" and the last syllable rhyming with "kite"), one would be just about right. One of Arthur's university professors—a nervous little man who immigrated to the United States before WWII—said there is no real translation for *Gemütlichkeit* and never would be. One has to experience *Gemütlichkeit*, he said, and maybe that could only be done in Germany. Arthur knows this difficult word has been translated as a warm feeling, a friendliness, or a sense of well-being. So, he's wondering if a little

Gemütlichkeit might actually be right here, in this dining room! Might the scent of *Gemütlichkeit*—left by some earlier guest—still linger here?

"Could it be at this table?" he wonders. "In the wood paneling? In the *air*?"

Looking at the two other restaurant customers, he wonders if they might have *Gemütlichkeit*. One is a distinguished-looking man and the other is a young boy. They are finishing their breakfast on the other side of the room. Arthur has seen them before, walking in the streets of Bad Aibling. The man is reading; the boy is writing, possibly to his mother. Arthur wonders why she isn't with them: Perhaps there are other children; or maybe she died giving birth. Is this a belated attempt of a busy father to get better acquainted with a sensitive or neglected son?

Continuing his speculation, Arthur wonders if, like so many visitors in Bad Aibling, one of them is hoping for a cure. The little village, with its alpine air and mud baths, offers a fashionable retreat for those needing a respite from the city. Arthur decides the slender boy is more likely to be ill. His father is also slender, but in him, it seems more natural. What have these thoughts to do with *Gemütlichkeit*? Arthur doesn't know.

As though expressly to interrupt his thoughts, the door of the hotel swings open, and an Arab youth, shoulders hunched up against the cold, enters the room. Arthur doesn't know him personally, but recognizes him as a fellow student at the Goethe Institute.

"*Grüss Gott*," Arthur says.

"*Grüss Gott*," replies the intruder, hanging his coat and scarf on a wrought-iron rack next to the door and taking a seat near a window.

Arthur knows only one of the Arabs, a young man named Hussein from Syria, soft-spoken and polite. Weeks ago, standing at one of the windows on the second floor of the institute, Arthur had watched students from Jordan, Egypt, and Lebanon throw snowballs and have a great time during the first snowfall of the season. For some of them, it was the first time they had ever seen real snow. As the dark colorful figures charged, retreated, pursued, attacked, lost balance, and fell in the snow, they had slowly turned into white warriors. He didn't know then, but soon would, that it was emblematic of future wars in the Middle East. What Arthur does know is that for them, Germany is even stranger than it is for him, a totally different physical, technological, and cultural climate.

As he is wondering about this, Arthur's thoughts are interrupted by the sound of music in the street. As it grows louder and louder, he quickly stands up, leaves some coins on the table, and takes his coat off the rack. The music is more distinct when he opens the first of the two hotel doors. Nonetheless, he is unprepared for the blast of sound that hits his ears as he opens the second door and steps out into the street. A parade is passing by!

Directly in front of Arthur and filling the street is a large band of elderly men in Bavarian costumes, playing a bizarre assortment of brass instruments, some unfamiliar to Arthur. Playing with much more gusto than precision, the musicians produce a deafening cacophony in the narrow street. Behind them, as far as Arthur can see, street and sidewalks are filled with villagers.

"What is this?" he asks of someone just outside the hotel.

"*Volkstrauertag*" (National Day of Mourning), he replies reproachfully.

Arthur wants to ask what this is about, but before he can, the man steps out into the crowded street behind the musicians. The parade turns out to be smaller than Arthur first imagined. The crowd behind the band is mostly elderly men and women, many with special Bavarian hats. After them, comes a smaller group of children sporting rosy cheeks and smiling faces. Arthur steps out into the street behind them, sometimes losing sight of the band as it leads the way through the winding streets.

After about ten minutes, the parade turns into a park at the edge of town, crosses a small bridge, and heads toward a life-size statue of a lion mounted on a large concrete pedestal. To either side of the lion, small bonfires sparkle in the recesses of the monument. The band leads the parade to the foot of the statue, then moves to one side, where it continues to play for several minutes. When they stop, a hatless man steps onto a platform in front of the lion and begins to speak.

Arthur, who hasn't crossed the bridge into the park, is unable to follow him word for word, but he catches enough to understand this ceremony is meant to honor men of the district who died in a war. Which war, he's not sure, but he hears the speaker remind the crowd of the senselessness of war. Arthur notices that, hats in hand, many in the audience listen with bowed heads, even some of the children. From time to time, a woman takes out a handkerchief and blows her nose or wipes her eyes. Arthur is reminded of Memorial Day at home, when he paraded down main street as part of a high-school band. There, he felt no great sorrow or pain as he certainly does here.

Arthur glances down at the water flowing by in a small canal under the bridge. It is clear and shallow. A large green vine passes by, rolling end over end in the current. When it moves toward a large craggy rock in the center of the stream, a collision is inevitable. He watches the vine bounce and squirm, then settle against the rock.

As the speech ends, the band strikes up a slow, sad song. Some old cannons are discharged once, twice, three times, as the musicians continue to play. When the last note is struck, the crowd begins to disperse. A muscular German youth is first to come away, glancing at Arthur as he crosses the bridge. Arthur stands in the cold, watching the crowd until only a few musicians, putting away their instruments, are left in front of the lion. Two workmen cross the bridge, lift the platform, and carry it away. Arthur glances back into the canal. The main body of the vine is still caught on the rock, but some of its longer branches, stretched full length by the strength of the water, extend well beyond the stone.

Sometime later, Arthur describes the parade in a letter to his family. And then he adds: "Wouldn't you know that, out of all the towns in Germany, I live in one with American soldiers! That's right, they're located just outside Bad Aibling! I met one last week. He told me they can't wear uniforms in town. That's why I haven't noticed them. He couldn't tell me about his job. Apparently, that's 'hush, hush.'

"This week I'm going to Vienna with an English student named Matthew. He knows a lot about history, so it should be educational. We'll leave on the 24th and my birthday is the 25th. So, I'll celebrate my twentieth birthday in Austria."

Two days later, Arthur goes to bed quite early, in anticipation of the two of them hitch-hiking their way toward Vienna early the next day. His bedside light is already off, when he hears a knock on the window. He sits up, pushes aside a curtain, and peers out. It's Matthew! Arthur makes a sign of recognition, snaps the light back on, pulls on pants and shoes, goes into the hallway, and opens the door.

"Very sorry to bother you," says Matthew, "but a telegram came for you at the institute."

"Come in!" Arthur replies. "I wasn't sleeping anyway." He takes the envelope from Matthew and leads him back into his room.

"Still snowing?"

"No, but jolly cold. I hope we won't see snow in Vienna."

Arthur tears open the telegram and reads it; then chuckles and reads it to Matthew: "*THANKS FOR LETTER. ENJOY VIENNA. HAPPY BIRTHDAY! MOM & DAD.*"

"I guess they figured I'd be off for Vienna before an ordinary letter could reach me."

"Good thing I was at the institute, or that message would have missed you." Then, for some reason, Matthew added: "Some of us were talking about the Wall in Berlin."

"What about the Wall?"

"It looks like it'll be there *forever*!"

7

More About Berlin and the Airlift

I GREW UP IN Lawton, Oklahoma, an Army town with soldiers everywhere. As a result, I had no interest in military service, especially the Army. So, when the federal government began drafting people into the Army, I signed up for Air Force Reserve Officers' Training Corps, which paid me (a little) and prepared me (somewhat) to be an Air Force officer. When I finished college, I went to Texas, where for many long months I was trained to be an intelligence officer. Then, they sent me to West Berlin to join a Security Service unit that used radar, electronic receivers, earphones, and some language training to track military planes flying in and around Berlin.

In part, we did this because Russian, East German, or Polish military planes would sometimes harass Western planes flying through one of three corridors to or from Berlin. It was important to know if provocations of this kind were done by the pilots themselves, or if they were ordered to do so by their ground controllers. We were also interested in any planes that somehow crossed the long border between East and West Germany. Some tried to do so purposely to get out of East Germany and into West Germany. For this reason, airfields in East Germany that were close to the border were for Russian pilots alone, lest some East German pilot decide to flee from the East into West Germany *by air*. On the other hand, many other pilots unknowingly flew from West Germany into East Germany, where they were sometimes shot down and killed, or forced to land and put in prison.

But I'm getting ahead of myself. In autumn of 1945, an Aviation Agreement was signed by all four countries occupying Germany. This created three air corridors for airplanes of western countries to reach Berlin. Those are the same corridors that made the Airlift possible, but they only had so much space. Each was 32 kilometers wide and 3,084 meters high. As a result, during the Airlift, planes often flew above and below one another at five different levels, usually in groups of ten or twelve at the same speed. This was somewhat dangerous, but made best use of what air space there was.

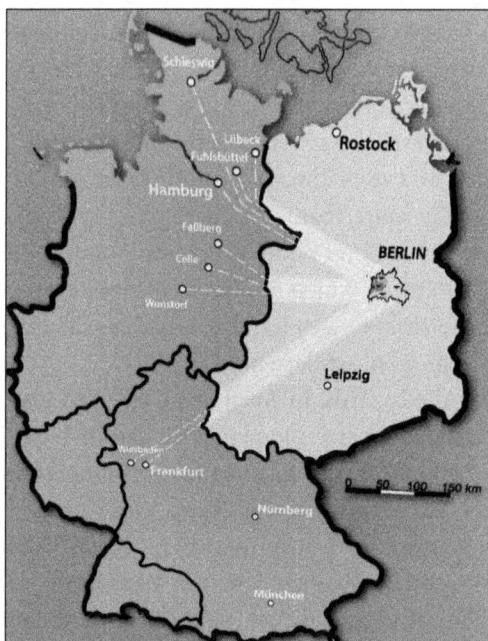

Three air corridors to Berlin
Graphic by Christian Nimpsch
© MHM Berlin-Gatow

37

At the end of 1946, the Western powers stopped delivering reparations to the Soviet Union, reparations for what the German military had done to Soviet infrastructure. The stop of reparations was done in part because the Soviets had not delivered food to West Berlin as agreed. On April 1, 1948, East Germans and Russians put all kinds of checks on trains going from West Germany to Berlin. The very next day, the United States chose to supply all their troops in West Berlin *by air.* Soon after, the British and the Americans decided to try to supply all of West Berlin—more than 2 million people—*through the air.* As a result, East German and Russian aircraft began to invade the three air corridors to harass (or to "buzz") aircraft bringing supplies to West Berlin.

On April 5, 1948, a Soviet fighter plane collided with a British passenger plane. The Soviet pilot and all fourteen in the other plane died in the crash. A second fatal accident occurred when a plane crashed into a house in West Berlin a few months later, killing pilot and co-pilot. According to the Air Force, more than a hundred fatalities were recorded during the Airlift, including 31 Americans and 40 Britons. According to an Air Force publication, there were more than a hundred cases where searchlights were used to try to blind pilots going into or out of Berlin, more than 170 incidents in which foreign airplanes flew too close, and more than 120 cases in which transports were subject to flak, air-to-air fire, or ground-artillery fire.[1]

Despite the hazards, in April 1949, a record was set: In one 24-hour period, almost 1,400 planes landed in West Berlin. According to *History.com,* a plane was taking off or landing in West Berlin every 30 seconds. At that point, more cargo was coming into Berlin than before the Communist blockade. During the Airlift, about 59,000 passengers flew into West Berlin and 166,000 flew out. American and British pilots flew 92 million miles in 278,228 flights. On the way in or out of the city, some parachuted packages of candy for the children of Berlin. No wonder many Berliners are so fond of their *air*!

---

1. Air Force News Service, June 26, 2023, 2

After about a year, it was clear that the Airlift could continue to feed and fuel Berlin indefinitely. For the Communists, it was a strategic disaster. Here is a perceptive paragraph from the Airlift Exhibition at Tempelhof:

> After the blockade and the Airlift, Berlin was also divided by the politics of remembrance. In the Western part, the notion of a city forced to starve emerged at a time of political confrontation during the Cold War. Its survival and freedom were accordingly due to the logistical feat of the Anglo-American Airlift alone . . . victors became protectors. This ideological characterization of West Berlin as a symbol of democracy and freedom lacked . . . a counterpart in the East German culture of remembrance. For East Germany, the failure of the blockade offered no reason for positive memories, while the continued existence of West Berlin was perceived as an unsolved problem.[2]

What was the "unsolved problem"? Well, there were many of them, some political, some practical. As an example of a practical one: Suppose you lived in East Berlin. To go to Potsdam on the other side of West Berlin, you would have to drive many hours to go around West Berlin to reach Potsdam. Why? Because the East German government would not allow you or any other ordinary citizen to go into or through West Berlin.

The Tempelhof exhibit also displayed an East German map of Berlin; but where West Berlin should have been, there is only white space. In East Germany, this was not unusual. Some maps made West Berlin look like a rural area by coloring it green. According to the Allied Museum in Berlin: "Beginning in 1964, East German guidelines dictated that published maps should be kept imprecise. From then on, towns and roads were drawn with deviations—in some case amounting to several kilometers from true—and the scale

---

2. The exhibition was a collaboration between the Military History Museum of the German Armed Forces Air Base Berlin-Gatow, the Allied Museum Berlin, and the Museum Berlin-Karlshorst.

of any given map often fluctuated. . . . . Every map went through a censor and had to be approved by the interior ministry."[3]

Unsolved problems drove the East German government into a state of paranoia. It was relentlessly spying on its own citizens and then making many of them spy on each other. As a result, little could happen without someone in the government knowing about it.

For East Germany and the Soviet Union, yet another political failure was still ahead. That was the building of the Berlin Wall in 1961, an attempt to keep East Germans and others from crossing from the Russian sector into West Berlin. I will have more to say about the Wall, but once again I'm getting ahead of myself.

As a result of the Berlin Airlift, all Soviet restrictions on train traffic to or from Berlin ended on 12 May, 1949. This also ended the Western countries' counter-blockade of goods going to the Soviet Union and East Berlin. Nonetheless, the Airlift continued for a while because of a railroad strike in West Berlin and to ensure the city would have enough food and fuel for several months.

Thus, the terror tactic of starving more than 2 million West Berliners so they would become part of East Germany did not work. It made many West Germans embrace democracy and the allied countries that won WWII.

Phased termination of the Airlift began in August 1949 and ended in early October. The Airlift was not exclusively American or British or military. Many Berliners and other civilians worked at various airports to support the Airlift. Thousands of Berlin civilians helped enlarge Tempelhof and Gatow Airports, even as others built a new Tegel Airport in the French sector of the city. In the meantime, American planes supplied both their own and the French sector of the city.

Was it expensive? Yes, of course. But compared to the annual expense of fighting WWII, it was relatively cheap. According to the *Encyclopaedia Britannica*, the Airlift cost $224 million and delivered more than 2 million tons of supplies, most of it coal. This does not include the cost of more than a hundred human lives.

---

3. From the Allied Museum's exhibition "100 Objects: Berlin during the Cold War"

8

Vienna, Nov. 25, 1961

"Matthew, are you sure you don't want to come along?"

"No, thank you, I'm spent," he says, looking up from a map spread out across the full width of his bed. "I'm plotting our itinerary for tomorrow."

"But, Matthew, this is our first night in Vienna; it's Saturday night, and it's my birthday!"

"Happy birthday!"

"But, Matthew, I'm twenty years old!"

"Congratulations, Arthur. You're almost an adult."

Arthur is also tired, but somehow energized by the thought of being twenty *at long last.* Matthew's sobriety does not dampen his enthusiasm and excitement.

"Matthew is an Englishman," Arthur thinks. "He will have other opportunities to visit Vienna. He's also a teenager. What does he know about nightlife?"

On his first of three nights in the Austrian capital, Arthur is hell-bent on making the most of it! He has no intention of staying in their bedroom, which was rented from a widow who saw them looking at ads in a nearby train station.

"I have lots of room, and good location" she had said in broken English. Not only that, their room came at a price they could not turn down, after paying for a train from Salzburg to Vienna.

After a begrudged *"Auf Wiedersehen"* (goodbye) to Matthew, Arthur picks up his overcoat and goes through a small sitting room, where he picks up a set of keys and lets himself out into the hallway. Taking stairs down to street level, he finds the door locked. He has to unlock it from the inside and then relock it from outside. It's part of being in Europe, Arthur thinks. "Back in Oklahoma, one doesn't think much about locking doors, even car doors!"

He comes out onto a small, narrow side street, which extends into darkness to his left and into misty neon brightness to his right. Heading towards the light, he decides to enter a small tavern. It's about nine o'clock, but not much is happening: just some old men, two of them playing chess. An overweight woman stands behind the counter. He starts to take a stool at the bar and watch the chess match, but changes his mind and walks across the room and out an opposite door onto a busy street with lots of cars but not many people.

"Jesus Christ," he thinks, "it's my birthday! I can't sit around watching people play chess, people I don't even know!" To his right, across a boulevard, he sees some massive buildings with lights revealing a long row of statues perched on top of them like guardian angels silhouetted in the sky.

"Nice," he says to himself. "Very nice."

He is curious about these buildings, and feels an urge to cross the street and see them up close. But he pauses, not knowing if it makes any sense to spend time looking at buildings in semi-darkness and in the cold, without a guide book and with no one to talk with. Tomorrow there would be plenty of time to see these sights.

Walking farther down the sidewalk, he walks between the architectural splendor on his right and the shop windows on his left. It's freezing cold, so his hands are in his pockets, despite the fact he thinks it improper.

"I've never seen one of them with their hands in their pockets. That's how they spot us Americans."

The night before, he had given his gloves to an Australian at a youth hostel in Salzburg. The bearded young man had played the guitar for them after dinner and described the year he spent in Barcelona learning to play flamenco.

Did the Australian like Spain? No, he hated it. "Worst place in the world to be without money," he said. He had to sleep in a flop house full of lice and fleas after his money ran out. Now, he was on his way back home, where he could earn a decent living. He had camped his way through the Alps with a bedroll and an umbrella after losing his gloves in a French hostel. Was he sorry he had gone to Spain?

"No! It's where you go to learn flamenco."

But something about the Australian bothers Arthur: How could anyone be unhappy in Barcelona?

Looking for some entertainment on his birthday, Arthur enters a cafe. After seating himself at a small table, he orders some coffee, and looks around him. "A bit too posh," he thinks, a phrase he picked up from Matthew. "Also, a bit modern. I must be right downtown."

There's something too familiar in the plate-glass windows, the Formica, the cash register . . . all too familiar, yet it is still somehow different. He feels the same nervous flutter in his stomach that he had at the sidewalk cafe in Rotterdam on his very first day in Europe.

This nervousness seems to follow him into all restaurants, cafes, bars, and coffee shops. Is this just a simple reaction to unusual surroundings? Many things here are different, of course, but that's no surprise. What is surprising is a feeling that *he* is different. "It's okay to feel like an intruder in a gothic cathedral or a rococo palace, but why feel that way *in a cafe?*" He then remembers his grandmother telling him her family was looked down on by some Texans, because her parents let her drink diluted coffee before she was six years old.

Before him on the table is a coffee service the waitress brought him with a polite *"Bitte schön."* Even the coffee service is different, especially the three paper-wrapped packages of sugar, two cubes to a package. But there is nothing *alien* about them.

Apparently, all the dinner guests have gone, and theatres and movies have not yet returned their crowds to the sidewalk. A murmur of conversation floats into his ears from a remote corner of the room, where a young couple are the only other customers. They seem to be about his age, but he can't say for sure because younger people in Europe seem to dress older, look older, act older.

"They are students on a date," he thinks, but he can't say for sure. They seem too calm and satisfied. "Yes, that is the part that is really strange: the *people.* Perhaps there's some big difference in their metabolism.

On a night out in Oklahoma, they would be at a movie, or dancing, or hot-rodding—not just *talking*!

Arthur wonders if he shouldn't try to join the couple. "It would be nice to talk a little German, find out where they're from, even ask what they've seen in Vienna." Nonetheless, he can't see himself actually doing that: How would he explain that he was out here alone on his twentieth birthday?

After leaving some money on the table and going outside, Arthur feels cold again. His feet had not warmed up. He wonders what he thought he would do out here after leaving Matthew in their warm bedroom? What did he expect to be so special? Did he think the Viennese would line the streets to celebrate his birthday?

Arthur considers going back to their rented room, but decides it's still too early. He imagines Matthew back in the bedroom, reading through guide books, deciding where they should go and marking each interesting spot on a map bought in the train station. Matthew is only eighteen and has not been to college, but he already knows some Latin and French. After only two months of private German studies in Munich, he is in the same class as Arthur, who has had three semesters of German at the University of Oklahoma!

Arthur's petty jealousy was soon diminished, however, under the pressure of a friendship which grew from the first day of class until they were planning a whole series of trips together. Nonetheless, it sometimes seems to Arthur that Matthew treats him like a child.

Finally, Arthur finishes his drink, pays the waiter, and returns to the street. The mist has turned to fog, and the street is coming to life. Couples in heavy overcoats stand impatiently at street corners, climb into deserted cars, or duck into welcoming cafes. Car traffic swells, tires squeal, lights flash on, voices float in the foggy air.

Aimlessly, he decides to explore some deserted streets, speaking the street names out loud. How long he wanders even he can't say. But eventually, he finds himself standing in front of a massive building shrouded in fog, which he takes to be a town hall, because a sign at one corner says *Ratskeller*, which he knows is something like a restaurant or a beer hall in a town-hall basement. As he walks toward the sign, a door flies open and he hears a blast of music and human voices. Without thinking, he moves through the doorway, down a flight of stairs, and into a very large restaurant.

The noisy panorama of the hall is so shocking, compared to the tranquility of the fog outside, that he feels like a stray creature in another world. It is one thing to enter something like this on purpose, expecting the grandeur and the gaiety of it all—watching it build, witnessing the transformation of a mausoleum into a din of festivity. It's quite another to stumble into it by chance, not as a participant, but as a solitary spectator.

The ceiling—high, high overhead—is barely visible through a thick cloud of smoke. The drone of the crowd, which reached him on the street, echoes inside like the roar of an engine. Between him and a small orchestra, he can dimly see row after row of long tables decked with elaborate decanters surrounded by large formal parties.

This is not the sort of place he would have picked, but feeling somehow committed now that he's inside, Arthur checks his coat and waits to be seated. Then, he follows a uniformed waiter the length of the restaurant to a small wooden table far from the entrance. Here, the waiter inquires condescendingly what he might want to order. *"Was möchte der junge Herr?"* (What might the young gentleman want?)

For a moment, Arthur is afraid the waiter is questioning his very presence in the hall. Then he orders a beer, but immediately regrets it. Nodding, as though confirming a suspicion, the waiter disappears, returning with a very tall mug, which he deposits on a cardboard coaster.

"Ein bier," he intones ceremoniously, then withdraws with a little bow. Behind the musicians is a colossal beer barrel, rising to a height way above the musicians and dominating one entire end of the cellar. Sipping his beer, Arthur surveys the much bigger tables around him. Here and there are some other small tables, but most of the crowd, as far as he can see, are seated at cloth-covered tables in groups of eight or twelve, each forming a small island of celebration in a sea of similar tables. No one, fortunately, pays him the slightest attention, yet he feels singularly out of place.

"What am I doing here?" he wonders. "I should go home and get some sleep." But he is tired and the beer is tasty. There is a slow thaw in his legs, his hands, his ears—everywhere but his feet, anchored on the cold, stone floor.

The music, which Arthur finds a bit tedious suddenly stops amid polite applause, but the echo of conversation continues. The musicians lay down their instruments and disperse, leaving behind three elderly violin players, who play what Arthur takes to be Slavic melodies.

The blast of the orchestra had resounded above and beyond the din of conversation, but these three string players are at first difficult to hear. Slowly but surely, however, the virtuosity of their playing begins to be noticed and a surprising hush begins at one end of the hall and runs like a rumor to the rear of the chamber. Soon, the musicians abandon the space in front of the barrel and begin to move in and out among the tables, asking for musical suggestions and playing all kinds of romantic requests.

Arthur is thrilled by the fiery rhythms and sometime passionate sadness of the trio. Was he in a large cave with some wandering gypsies? Any moment now, he expects to see a dark-skinned maiden begin to dance and sing with billowing skirts, stiletto heels, and challenging eyes. Raising the earthen mug to his lips, Arthur tilts back his head and drains it to the bottom.

At the end of one such tune, the trio begins moving up the aisle toward Arthur. When they stand in front of him, they bow to generous applause. As they start to return to the open space in front of the barrel, Arthur applauds wildly, and one of the musicians gives him a grateful nod of the head. In response, Arthur raises his hand high above his head in a gesture of tribute. But to Arthur's great surprise, the violinist starts walking back towards him with a grateful smile. Next, with a stiff bow, the musician says something in German which is incomprehensible to Arthur, and the violinist seems to be listening for a reply.

Suddenly, to Arthur, it seems terribly quiet in the great hall, as though everyone were listening. All he can think to say is *"Wie bitte?"* (What did you say?)

"I have asked you," comes the reply in perfect English, *"What would you like us to play?"*

Arthur feels a hot wave of embarrassment. He has been found out! He had not wanted to make a musical request, but now it came to him that he *must* do so. He can't remember the name of anything appropriate, but suddenly, he thinks of one of his favorite tunes. The

English-speaking musician repeats the name of the song to the other two players, as they surround Arthur's table. Then they tuck their instruments under their chins with great care and begin with the dramatic, romantic song:

April in Paris!

To Arthur, it seems the song goes on for hours, not minutes. It's as if a spotlight were shined on him, seated alone in a large hall filled with properly dressed grown-ups, who were perhaps having a good laugh at his expense.

At the end of the song, Arthur pays for his beer and walks away with as much dignity as possible, first to the coat room and then the exit, wondering why he had ventured out into the streets of Vienna.

"I don't feel like a foreigner," he says to himself, "I feel like a refugee!" The word "refugee" lingers in Arthur's head as he goes out the door. He knows back in Oklahoma there's a refuge for buffalo. "Could there be a refuge," he wonders, "for people like me?"

He didn't feel at home in Oklahoma, and now he doesn't seem to fit in here. People his own age seem more mature, even younger people like Matthew! Is Arthur caught up somewhere *in between*?

9

When Is One a Berliner?

Much of what I say about the Airlift comes from the Airlift Exhibition at Tempelhof. The year 2023, when I returned to Berlin, was not only the 75th anniversary of the Airlift; it was also the 60th anniversary of the speech President Kennedy made in Berlin on June 26, 1963, just some months before he was shot and killed. His speech included that charming phrase: *"Ich bin ein Berliner!"* (I am a Berliner!).

To put that in context, the former President said: "All free men, wherever they may live are citizens of Berlin. And therefore, as a free man, I take pride in the words, *Ich bin ein Berliner.*" Kennedy wanted Berliners to know he was as interested in their city as they were and that they could rely on him to keep West Berlin free from the Communists who surrounded them. On July 13, 2023, I read in *Berliner Zeitung* (Berlin Newspaper) a column by Jens Blankennagel titled *"Wann Ist man Berliner?"* (When Is One a Berliner?).

> Berlin is a city of immigrants. Some, like me, come from Aschersleben, others from Augsburg or Anatolia or

Arizona. . . . what kind of city would Berlin be, if more than 54 percent of the population were missing?"[1]

Perhaps, instead of declaring: *"Ich bin ein Berliner,"* I could just say "I'm at home in Berlin." This brings to mind the German word *Fernweh,* which means something like wanting to be somewhere else or far-sickness, the opposite of homesickness. In Oklahoma, I used to feel something like *Fernweh.* I had a hankering to be somewhere else. Is that why so many "new Berliners" come to this city? Is Berlin something of a magnet for people like me, especially artists, writers, and other curious people willing to take a little or a lot of risk?

Berlin is certainly full of artists. My wife and I met one of them just before we left Berlin. While we were looking at her paintings and chatting back and forth with Susanne Rikus, she suggested we film our conversation. I opted out, but my wife and Susanne recorded a brilliant conversation, which can be seen at *marielaureauthor.com.* Susanne is from West Germany, but many Berlin artists were not born in Germany. A few days after I left the city, I read this article by Clarissa Rios in *Berlin Without Borders:*

> Berlin has long served as an artistic hub, welcoming creative people from all over the world. Its thriving art scene can be traced back to the 1920s Weimar era. Again, in the early 1990s after the Berlin Wall opened, artists, musicians, and writers flocked to Berlin from around the globe. It's a city that boasts the avant-garde spirit and creative energy that artists yearn for. The exiles and refugees of recent years have only enhanced that reputation . . . . Among the large immigrant and refugee populations in Germany are many artists, musicians, performers, and other creatives. They have formed artist collectives, opened galleries, and brought the cultural and social life they left behind to Berlin. Though they may be reluctant to admit that exile is a mixed blessing, many thrive in Berlin's vibrant and tolerant atmosphere.[2]

1. *Berliner Zeitung,* Number 160, Thursday, 13 July, 2023, 4
2. *Berlin Without Borders,* 9 August, 2023.

The truth about Berlin is that this city is more open-minded than most other cities in Germany, and maybe in Europe. Before 1990 and the reunification of East and West Germany, West Berliners were exempt from the military draft, as the city did not formally belong to the Federal Republic of Germany. Back then, many West Germans did not want to live in Berlin, because it was so far away and surrounded by East Germany. Nonetheless, some moved to Berlin immediately on high-school graduation to avoid the draft or alternative service. I think this helped fill Berlin with younger, perhaps more progressive people.

10

Bad Aibling, Dec. 10, 1961

His Bavarian landlady wakes Arthur up from a deep sleep. He doesn't often hear her tending a stove in the hall, but a glance at his watch tells him it's half-past nine on a cold Sunday morning. During the week, she does this after he goes to the Goethe Institute, then again in the early afternoon before he returns. Extending an arm from the warmth of the eiderdown, he reaches for his handkerchief on a bedside table. Prying it apart, he carefully selects a clean, dry portion and blows his nose.

Putting the handkerchief back on the table, Arthur pulls his feet up under the covers, resuming the fetal position dictated by the size of the eiderdown. He delays getting out of bed because it's freezing in his room. Through a nearby window, Arthur can see it will be another grey and drizzly day.

He shares the hall toilet and stove with another student living in a room identical to his. During the week, he must be up before dawn to get to the institute in time for breakfast. Today he can stay in bed until the room warms up, or perhaps spend the whole morning in bed. But he will have to get dressed to go to the toilet, as the widow who lives upstairs also uses the hallway to get in and out of the house. For Arthur, the thought of staying in bed seems very pleasant, maybe even *gemütlich*.

In Arthur's grammar book, there is a picture at the top of a page that introduces the word *Gemütlichkeit*. On an impulse, he picks up the book from the table and turns to that page. Although he has seen it many times, he stares at the photo again as though seeing it for the first time:

A middle-aged couple is seated before a small fireplace in large upholstered armchairs. Both are a bit overweight. The man is impeccably dressed in coat and tie, his collar straight and stiff. However, a flamboyant handkerchief peeks from his breast pocket. He is almost completely bald, but sports a carefully trimmed goatee and mustache. He is reading a newspaper, and a thin line of smoke rises from a pipe on the table beside him.

The woman, eyes closed, wears a shapeless dress with a very elaborate collar. It extends in a large V down to a button at her breast. Her left elbow rests in her right hand, allowing her left forefinger to stroke or perhaps support her chin. Her neck is separated from her chest by a string of pearls, and her crossed legs rest on a padded footstool. On the mantel between the married couple is a radio and on the floor is a young, healthy dachshund, his friendly eyes staring from the book at every reader. This makes Arthur smile, because the dog reminds him of hot dogs, which some German-Americans call "dachshund sausages."

In the textbook below the photo, Arthur reads something like the following in German:

It's Sunday. The couple and their son have just returned from church. The father is reading; she is listening to music from a radio. The boy's friends are away on holiday. What can he do? The dachshund is also his friend. They can't talk very much; the dog doesn't have a big vocabulary. But he shows his feelings by wagging his tail, shaking his head, or barking. Some say he is ugly, but that's not true. He is a perfect German dachshund.

The boy takes the dog for a walk along a nearby river. Once in a while, he throws a piece of wood into the water and the dog retrieves it. Later on, when the dog meets other dogs, the boy sits down on a bench to read a story book. Before he knows it, it's getting dark. So, he calls the dog, and they go home together, thinking that it was, after all, *ein gemütlicher Tag* (a pleasant day).

This reminds Arthur of a German proverb:

In Geldsachen, hört die Gemütlichkeit auf.

(Where money begins, pleasantries end.)

Arthur closes the book, wondering if "pleasantries" is a good translation—and whether he will ever experience genuine *Gemütlichkeit*.

PART II

Terroristador

11

Why I Came Back to Berlin

I WANTED TO REMEMBER what had happened there and how Germans are dealing with the past: Why someone burned the *Reichstag* (parliament building) and how Adolf Hitler came to power. Does public apathy help mobsters commit their most heinous crimes?

For many years, Hitler was a comical figure, saying audacious things that few Germans believed. In 1923, he was found guilty of treason for leading the Munich Beer Hall Putsch, an attempted coup. As a result, he was sentenced to five years in prison, a very short sentence from a sympathetic judge. Nonetheless, had he served the full five years, the history of the 20th century might have been completely different. *Hitler was released after nine months!*

In 1925, Hitler published *Mein Kampf* (*My Struggle*), a book he wrote in prison. That same year, Hitler created the *Schutzstaffel* (Protection Squads), otherwise known as the SS. They were initially only bodyguards, but became policemen and much more in what Hitler called the Third Reich (the third German empire). The first endured about a century; the second, a half century. The so-called Third Reich lasted only twelve years, half of them during WWII, which took the lives of some 8 million Germans.

The SS had only about 300 members until 1929, when Heinrich Himmler took over and expanded it. By 1933, the SS had grown to more than 50,000 bellicose people chosen for racial purity, blind obedience, and their loyalty to Hitler.

In the presidential election of 1932, Hitler got a little more than 36 percent of the vote. President Paul von Hindenburg received more than 53 percent. Hindenburg appointed Hitler as chancellor of Germany in 1933, but Hitler was not yet in full power. In the same year, Hindenburg helped pass the *Reichstag* Fire Decree, which curtailed some personal liberties and rights, even though the cause of the *Reichstag* fire was never fully explained. Then Hitler proposed the Enabling Act of 1933. When this became law, Hitler was given power to override individual rights in the German Constitution. Now, the SS could do what they wanted to do *legally*. In August 1934, following the death of Hindenburg, Hitler merged the chancellery with the presidency to become the *Führer* (the one Leader) of Germany.

In March 1938, Hitler assaulted, annexed, and took over Austria, the country where he was born. Most people in both countries supported the invasion. November 9 of that year is called *Kristallnacht* (Night of Broken Glass). Almost a hundred people were killed by the Nazis and thousands of Jewish businesses vandalized. Thousands of Jews were arrested and taken to concentration camps. *Kristallnacht* led to the killings of millions of Jews by the Nazis during the Holocaust.

Who was responsible for all this? Adolf Hitler.

When I first heard of the Holocaust, I did not believe it. How could the Nazis have murdered so many people while they were fighting and eventually losing WWII. It just didn't make sense to me. In hindsight, I can see that for Hitler the Holocaust was very important. Why? Because of all the people in Germany, it would have been the Jews who would have protested the most against his glorified war.

After I left the Goethe Institute, I went to the University of Frankfurt, where I was interrogated by three administrators about whether I knew enough German to be a student there. I must have learned a lot at the Goethe Institute, because they decided in my favor. I signed up for classes in history, philosophy, and literature, including one about how the Nazis came to power. What I most remember is that the Nazis used fear and intimidation to keep other people from speaking out or trying to help anyone the Nazis persecuted.

I got insight into this after I rented a little room in an apartment where an elderly German couple lived. One day two policemen came to question me about an automobile accident. Since I was not there, my landlords were questioned instead. When I returned, they were panic-stricken. It made no difference *why* they had come to their apartment; my landlords were terrorized just to have *policemen enter their home!* They feared for their lives because they lived through so many years of Nazi terror.

Do you remember the elderly couple Arthur read about in his German grammar book? How they were so relaxed and satisfied on a Sunday after coming home from church? They were full of *Gemütlichkeit*. My landlords in Frankfurt had definitely lost any *Gemütlichkeit* they may have had prior to Hitler coming to power and his brutal war.

Why was I living in a little room in a little apartment in Frankfurt? Because I was running out of money. After about two months at the Goethe Institute, I lived with my brother and his family in Darmstadt, a city south of Frankfurt. As an Air Force officer, he suggested I seek a job at *Stars and Stripes*, a newspaper for the American military. I did get a job there—not as a writer—but washing dishes in a cafe.

One of the first days I worked there, an elderly woman (who reminded me of my grandmother) asked me how much I was being paid. I told her the amount, which wasn't much. But a short time later, when an Army colonel came to inspect the kitchen, she cried out and complained to him that I was making more than she was, after working there for years!

The colonel told me I was a traitor to our country. I didn't know what to say back. Later, I learned the American military could only hire German civilians at certain salaries, lest it employ all the best people in the country. While I was in Darmstadt, I also worked for Röhm und Haas, a chemical company that hired me and many Italian immigrants to move plexiglass sheets from one place to another. Finally, I got a job at the Darmstadt Officer's Club. A few years later, I would live for more than a year at the Officers Club in Tempelhof.

Hitler wanted Tempelhof to be an airport that would reflect the power of the Nazis and the glory of Germany. And Tempelhof is full of a kind of glory, beginning with the Knights Templar, who gave Tempelhof its name. For about two medieval centuries, the Templars were a Catholic military order that combined monastic life with defending what they called holy places.

During WWII, Tempelhof was used as a factory for building military planes and weapons (sometimes with forced labor). The airport was only finished after the United States took it over, following the surrender of Germany in 1945. In 2023, the edifice was filled with more than a hundred tenants or organizations, as my wife, daughter, and I discovered when we ducked into the building to get out of the rain and suddenly found ourselves in Sigmund Freud University.

More than anything, I think of the Nazis as racists. They saw themselves as defenders of the Aryan race. When Aryan-race theory became part of Nazi ideology, the word Aryan meant whatever Hitler and the SS wanted it to mean. Those who joined the SS were racially screened, and if they seemed to have Slavic, Negroid, or Jewish racial features they were refused. Some had to prove they had only Aryan ancestors back to 1750, according to the *Holocaust Encyclopedia.*[1]

It took many years for Hitler to become *Führer,* but he seemed to know all one needs is the right propaganda—that if you continue to say things that are untrue loud enough and long enough (using modern media), many people will begin to believe what is untrue and then begin to believe in *you.* At first, many made fun of Hitler. But over time, as he became powerful, it became difficult to think of him that way. This is something Germans know more than we do: That a minority in any country can take freedom away from the majority through lies, terror, and resulting fears.

1. Website, United States Holocaust Museum

The following poem calls Adolf Hitler a *terror-ist'-a-dor,* a word I created to rhyme with *dic'-ta-tor. (Ideally, lines indented are for a second voice; words in the last line are for both voices.)*

Terror-ist-a-dor

Hitler first became a *terror-ist-a-dor,*
    a *terror-ist-a-dor,*
so, he could be a *dic-ta-tor,*
    a *dic-ta-tor.*

The world is full of *dic-ta-tors,*
    who first of all were *terror-ist-a-dors.*
A *dic-ta-tor* is first of all a *terror-ist-a-dor,*
    then a *dic-ta-tor,*
& last of all a *tyrant,* a *tyrant,*
    a *tyrant-a-dor!*

Many millions of innocents killed
    people killed, people killed,
so other folks would then obey,
    would then obey.
What Mussolini, Hitler, & Stalin did
    decades, decades ago,
now Putin, Xi, & others are doing
    while you read this little poem.

Hitler did not want to be
    an *ad-min-is-tra-dor,*
he wanted to be a *dic-ta-tor*
    a *dic-ta-tor* "some" would adore.

A *dic-ta-tor* is first of all
   a *terror-ist-a-dor;*
then a *dic-ta-tor*, a *dic-ta-tor*,
   & last of all a *tyrant-a-dor,*
a *tyrant-a-dor*, a *tyrant-a-dor*,
   or perhaps a *mat-a-dor,*
a *mat-a-dor*, a *mat-a-dor*,
   the bloody one who kills the bull!

Do you want to see what Adolf Hitler was like? Then you should see *Der Untergang* (*Downfall*). This 2004 German-Austrian-Italian movie was a 2005 Oscar nominee for Best Foreign Language Film. It's about the last days of the Nazi dictator, after he retreated to a large bunker not far from the *Reichstag.* The movie is based on at least two books: *Inside Hitler's Bunker: The Last Days of the Third Reich* by historian Joachim Fest and *Until the Final Hour* by Traudl Junge, a Hitler secretary in the bunker. The movie shows just how mesmerized were the people around Hitler, even though he was nearly insane and denying reality until the very end. Be forewarned though, this film is long (more than two and a half hours) and full of violence.

In July of 2023, my wife and I stood in front of what was once Adolf Hitler's great bunker (*Führerbunker*), now fully buried in the ground. I felt a little disappointed, because there was so little left to see. Nonetheless, I was glad to know where the bunker is and where Hitler and his wife committed suicide on 30 April, 1945, one day after they were married and just a week before the end of the war.

In very striking contrast, one of the most interesting buildings we saw in Berlin was the restored *Schönhausen Palace* on *Tschaikowski Strasse* in what was East Berlin. *Schönhausen* and its neighborhood are still intact, because this part of Berlin was not bombed out like many parts of the city.

Schönhausen Palace
Photo by Marie Laure

Schönhausen has a magical ballroom, beautiful stairways, some luxurious furnishings, and wonderful gardens. But, like the *Führerbunker*, it is the ugly things that happened there that fascinated us. For instance, from 1740 to 1797, it was the summer residence of Queen Elisabeth Christine, the wife of Frederick the Great. The Prussian Queen was disrespected by her husband and his family. After his ascent to the throne, his wife was not allowed to take part in his life. She lived in Berlin—in summer at

Schönhausen, the rest of the year at Berlin Palace. Her husband lived in Potsdam, just outside Berlin.

In the 20th century, *Schönhausen* became a depot for what Nazis called "degenerate art." Several thousand confiscated artworks were stored at *Schönhausen;* some were sold for foreign currency. Any artwork that seemed "modern" was condemned. Do you remember the photo of a woodcut print I talked about at the beginning of this book—the one I think of as two women who had lost a husband or father during WWII? That is an expressionist piece of modern art, and Germany is famous for such art and artists. Many of them became expressionists by reacting to the horrors of war, and for that reason their art can be very emotional.

After WWII, *Schönhausen* became interim quarters for the Soviet Military Administration and then official residence of Wilhelm Pieck, president of East Germany from 1949 to 1960. At that time, the palace was surrounded by perimeter walls and sentry stations. In 1960, *Schönhausen* became the seat of *Staatsrat der DDR* (State Council of the German Democratic Republic, a kind of collective head of state controlled by the Social Democratic Party of Germany.)

Later, the building was used as a guest house for visiting dignitaries, including Leonid Brezhnev, General Secretary of the Communist Party of the Soviet Union; Cuban President Fidel Castro; Muammar Gaddafi, the de-facto leader of Libya; Yasser Arafat, President of the Palestinian National Authority; Nicolae Ceausescu, President of Romania; and last of all by Mikhail Gorbachev, final leader of the Soviet Union.

12

Berlin in 2023

THE YEAR 2023 WAS not only the 60th anniversary of President Kennedy's speech in Berlin (and his untimely assassination), but also the 90th anniversary of Hitler coming to power. I was not expecting to see the Airlift Exhibition at Tempelhof. I did not even know until I was back in Berlin that 2023 was the 75th anniversary of the Airlift. So, when I ran into the exhibition, it surprised and fascinated me.

But to some, the exhibit might have been a disappointment. Here is part of a review by Kamiel Vermeulen, a young journalist from the Netherlands. According to his July 9 article in *Berlin Beyond Borders,* he was less excited about the exhibit than I was:

> Considering that this exhibition honors 75 years since that crucial Allied air operation, it is underwhelming. Five detached walls make up the exhibition, each with some text blocks and pictures on it. There are a few buttons you can press to hear some audio fragments, but it doesn't get any more interactive than that. Together with a lack of color, it makes it hard to imagine that the exhibition would interest a new generation in the historical significance of the Berlin Airlift. Just a few decades ago, East Berliners enjoyed few of the freedoms they do today.

As someone born this century, I find it near impossible to imagine what this would be like . . . . But [the exhibition] feels like a missed opportunity, a place where young Berliners could have been reminded of things they take for granted today.[1]

Entrance to Tempelhof Exhibition about Berlin Airlift

How did I come to see the Airlift Exhibition? I was returning after many decades to Tempelhof, where I had worked from 1965 to '68. If I had known about it, I would have tried to be at Tempelhof to see the opening of the exhibit. But on June 27, I walked with my daughter and wife along *Hasenheide Strasse*, then through a large park to Tempelhof, despite some rain and wind that demolished my umbrella.

I mentioned *Hasenheide Strasse* because in 1967 and '68 that is where we lived—me, my first wife, and our daughter, Laura, who was born in Berlin. That apartment building no longer exists. Even when we rented an apartment there, half the edifice was already bombed out. To cope with cold weather, we had two

1. *Berlin Beyond Borders*, July 9, 2023

cockle-stoves and a hot-water heater, all of them fired by coal. To take a bath, one had to light a fire under the hot-water heater and then burn some coal. After a couple of hours, the water would be warm enough for someone to get into the tub.

Author/daughter on *Hasenheide Str.*
Photo by Marie Laure

Although I had worked there decades earlier, it was only when I saw the Tempelhof exhibit that I realized the importance of the Airlift, the enormous size of Tempelhof, and that its runways had not been used for more than a decade! Construction of the airport began in the 1920s. When the Nazis came to power, it was expanded into one of the largest buildings in the world. A digital publication called *CNET* has described it as "a labyrinth that sprawls across a bewildering 3.2 million square feet and 9,000 rooms."[2]

In a 2014 referendum, Berliners rejected a plan to build on Tempelhof airfield, preferring instead to use the former airport as a huge inner-city park. Covering more than 800 acres, it is about the size of Central Park in New York City.

Germany has had an eagle on its coat of arms for centuries. Hitler kept the Weimar eagle for two years, then replaced it with a black eagle above a swastika. This may explain why so many eagles were built into the face of Tempelhof. This oval building was apparently designed to resemble an eagle in flight. And there is still a statue of an eagle's head in front of what is called Eagle Square, the main entrance to Tempelhof.

An eagle on Tempelhof building

2. CNET, September 15, 2017

When I returned to Berlin in 2023, we rented an apartment on *Kollwitz Strasse* in a neighborhood that had been part of East Berlin, so we were not expecting very much. However, it turned out to be a wonderful place, full of cafes, restaurants, bakeries, and coffee shops. Twice a week, we enjoyed a marvelous farmer's market just outside our building!

Kollwitz Strasse is named after Käthe Kollwitz, an important anti-war artist, who lived there until 1943. Her home was bombed and destroyed after she left Berlin. There is a bronze sculpture of Kollwitz by Gustav Seitz in a park named after Kollwitz just a block from where we lived. We were hoping to see some of Kollwitz' artwork, but the Käthe Kollwitz Museum was closed for renovations.

We were particularly interested in art museums. To save money, we bought relatively inexpensive three-day passes for the ones on Museum Island. Unfortunately, there is much more to these museums than anyone can see in just three days. This is a problem for all the city's main museums: They are way too big for ordinary tourists, even those staying in Berlin for *forty days*! Yes, most of them are beautiful and seldom boring, but for us they were almost always exhausting. While we were on Museum Island, we took a one-hour cruise on the Spree River and saw many of Berlin's charming buildings from a completely new and sparkling perspective.

Our second day in Berlin, having seen Tempelhof the day before, we went to *Brandenburger Tor,* which is surrounded by foreign embassies. This *Tor* (gate or door) still stands, but the nearby Wall which divided West Berlin from East Berlin is no longer there. The late-eighteenth-century *Brandenburger Tor* is now a symbol of peace and unity. But according to a document given us as we entered *Raum der Stille* (Room of Silence) at *Brandenburger Tor:* "In the wake of World War II—and even more so as the Berlin Wall was built along it in 1961—the Brandenburg Gate was the symbol of a divided city and a divided world."[3] Now it is a symbol of peace, as it was supposed to be. In the Room of

3. See www.raum-der-stille-im-brandenburger-tor. de

Silence, visited by some 70,000 people a year, one can relax, pray, or meditate. To me, Room of Silence speaks of *Gemütlichkeit;* where *Gemütlichkeit* is, all is peace.

Brandenburger Tor
Photo by Marie Laure

Most of the Berlin Wall has disappeared, but there are many places where you can still see pieces of it. I was not interested in the Wall; I had many views of it while I lived in Berlin. So, we didn't go to the East Side Gallery, which then had the longest continuous section of the Wall. Some 118 artists from 21 countries had painted this section of the Wall and turned it into an open-air exhibit. I'm sorry we missed it—not to see the Wall, but for the art.

Another thing that has changed in Berlin is the food served in restaurants. It's much better than when I was there before. Then, many served German meals. Now there are fewer of those and many more dishes from the Middle East, Northern Africa, Asia, and the rest of Europe—plus, of course, hamburgers from America.

Some of our most delicious meals were in cafes or restaurants near our apartment. Our most unforgettable meals were at the *Literaturhaus* (Literature House) and the *Teehaus im Englishen Garten* (English Tea House). They are not far from each other; the former is near the street called *Kurfürstendamm*, the latter in *Tiergarten*, a big park in central Berlin. Also nearby is the tall *Siegessäule* (Victory Column) in the middle of *Tiergarten*. I foolishly walked all the way to the top, more than 200 feet, but when I came back down, I could barely walk! If you want to see more of the *Siegessäule*, you should see Der *Himmel über Berlin* (The Sky over Berlin).

In English, it's called *Wings of Desire*, a 1987 film with Bruno Ganz and Peter Falk. Falk playing the fictional Columbo *in a German movie*? Yes, he does, and he seems to enjoy being in perhaps the best film ever made about this city. I also like the fact that Peter Handke, a German poet, helped write the script, which is full of poetry.

My wife and I found our way around Berlin slowly but surely by subway (U-Bahn and S-Bahn), or by bus and tram. All were included in monthly tickets we bought. Some buses were double-deckers, and they reminded me of a long-ago shock—a shock that came on a double-decker while I was still in the Air Force and not yet married. Late one evening, as I returned to Tempelhof by bus, I fell asleep on the upper deck. When I awoke, I was all alone up there! There was no one else that I could see or ask. There was no driver up front and no one behind, but the bus was still rolling on! I could not explain what I was seeing, *so I thought I was going straight to hell!*

On another day years ago, I stayed too long on the S-Bahn and suddenly I was passing heavily guarded "ghost stations" in

East Berlin, where no one could get on or get off. It was particularly scary for me because of my top-secret security clearance: I had been strictly told to stay out of East Berlin, so I was greatly relieved when we got back into West Berlin.

We arrived in Berlin on the 26th of June and left the 3rd of August. As a result, we did not see or hear any performance of the *Deutsche Oper Berlin*, the city's largest opera house, or the *Berlin Philharmonie*. We had hoped to hear the *Philharmonie* play Berlin's unofficial anthem *"Berliner Luft"* (Berlin Air). But we were able to attend the season's last concert at *Staatsoper Berlin*, the State Opera on a street called *Unter den Linden* (Under the Linden Trees). Before we went to the concert, we ate outside at a cafe on *Unter den Linden*. It was hard to believe I was actually sitting there after so many decades of wanting to see this famous street. If you go to Berlin, you don't want to miss it. It is near the *Reichstag*, just east of *Brandenburger Tor*.

Because of its iconic role in German history, it seems logical that the *Reichstag* should have the city's most extraordinary tourist attraction. You can go up to its huge glass dome in a very large and modern elevator. It lets you out on the roof, right above the plenary chamber, where you can see but not hear what is being debated. It was designed that way to suggest transparency. This glass dome is wonderful, not just for its design, but for its gracious views of Berlin and for some headphones, which tell you exactly what you're viewing in every direction.

Inside the glass dome
Photo by Marie Laure

My wife noticed our neighborhood didn't have many church-
es, yet bells persistently rang out seven days a week at regular
intervals. She was curious to know what denomination was following such strict prayer cycles. One evening, as we searched for
a restaurant, we heard and saw a soaring bell tower straight ahead

of us on *Schönhauser Allee*. The gates were open, but *Stadtkloster Segen* church was closed. So, we picked up some brochures.

After having the brochures translated, my wife realized this was just the kind of place she had hoped to find while away from home. The small community of non-ordained women and men worked, lived, and prayed together on a schedule that rivaled any monastery she had ever visited. The prayer day began at 8 a.m. and finished at 8 p.m. The bells call anyone passing by to stop and enjoy, which we certainly did.

13

Contrition

Berlin is full of contrition,
first step toward conciliation.
Reminders here are everywhere.
Most Berliners are contrite, I swear,
that it seems capital of a sinning nation.
Contrition will break down self-delusions
& trigger a reaction that can be pure as Love.
Most of Americans seem diametrically opposite,
more prepared to fight than be a little more contrite.

To ME, THE CHANGE in Berliners from old to new (from 1960s to 2020s) comes in part from contrition. Why do I speak of Berliners and their contrition? Because the city is so full of it! Berliners know things done before and during WWII were brutal and wrong. There are memorials to that everywhere: A large memorial to the Nazi genocide of Sinto and Roma peoples, a large Memorial to the Murdered Jews of Europe (the Holocaust Memorial), many Berlin Wall memorials, a Freedom Memorial to victims of the Berlin Wall, three Russian War Memorials, and I don't know how many *Stolpersteine* (literally, stumbling stones).

One corner of Holocaust Memorial
Photo by Marie Laure

A *Stolperstein* is a ten-centimeter concrete cube with a brass plate inscribed with names and life dates of victims of Nazi persecution. They are put in front of last homes or work places those people freely chose. The word *Stolperstein* reminds me of what someone said while we were eating dinner at the Literature House: "People here are tripping over their history every single day."

There is also a Memorial to Homosexuals Persecuted under the Nazis. Germany outlawed homosexuality in the 1950s and '60s, reformed the law in '69 and '73, and finally revoked it in '94. A large homosexual community has been very active in Berlin for more than a century, except perhaps when the Nazis were in power.

Neue Wache (New Guard) is an early 19th-century building on *Unter Den Linden*. It was originally a guardhouse for the Royal Palace, but became a memorial for those who died in the Napoleonic Wars and Wars of Liberation. Since 1993, it has been home for Käthe Kollwitz' sculpture *Mother with her Dead Son*. Kollwitz lost two sons during WWI.

I know there is much more to be said about Berlin memorials, but I think this is enough to make my point: There are many of them and they are always reminding Berliners of awful things that happened not so long ago—*in their own city* and almost everywhere in Europe.

I had a similar feeling when watching the American movie *Oppenheimer* as it premiered in Berlin. The film is about J. Robert Oppenheimer, sometimes called the "father of the atomic bomb." The large theatre in our neighborhood was packed on July 20 at 4 p.m., the movie's opening day. We know it was crowded, because we bought the last two tickets!

Toward the end of the movie, Oppenheimer says he wished he had developed the atomic bomb more quickly, so it could have been used against Germany. There was no screaming or anything like that—just a hush as the movie went on, but it took my breath away. The film won seven Academy Awards for best picture, director, actor, supporting actor, film editing, score, and cinematography.

I tried to read or scan at least one German newspaper each day from Monday to Friday for about six weeks. If I had done that every single day with every Berlin newspaper, I might have seen nothing else. Here are some of the contrition-related articles that interested me:

Most Berlin newspapers were reporting on *Mohren Strasse* (Street of the Moors). The issue was whether its name should or would be changed. As a part of denazification after WWII, many street names associated with the Nazis had been changed, but the name *Mohren Strasse* had not been changed. In fact, an East Berlin subway station once called *Otto Grotewohl Strasse* (after the first prime minister in East Germany) was renamed *Mohren Strasse* in 1991, after reunification of East and West Germany.

A court decided the street name could be changed if the district wanted. The name was changed to *Anton-Wilhelm-Amo Strasse*, in honor of the first student of African descent to study at a Prussian university. As justification for renaming *Mohren Strasse,* two Berlin political parties, the Greens and the Social Democrats, said: "According to today's understanding of democracy, the existing racist core of the name is burdensome and damages Berlin's international reputation."[1]

Of course, racism is still a problem around the world. The *Berliner Zeitung* of July 19, 2023, informed me that Jeremy Osborne—a black man born in America, but then part of the *Deutsche Oper Chor* (German Opera Choir)—was discriminated against and attacked by four people working for the *Verkehrsbetriebe*, Berlin's public transportation company. As a result, a judge ordered the *Verkehrsbetriebe* to pay Osborne 1,000 euros as compensation.

Germany's colonial past is still to be reckoned with. Other articles made it clear that the provenance of archaeological collections in Berlin's National Museums will be reviewed because of acquisition policies dating back to German colonialism. Museums will approach other countries to develop suitable solutions, which might include return of the objects.

This is from an article in the *Berliner Zeitung* of 4 July 2023: "No country has more objects from Cameroon in its museums than Germany."[2] In a document called *Atlas of Absence—Cameroon's Cultural Heritage in Germany*, it is said that Germany once controlled territory in more than a dozen African countries;

1. *Berliner Zeitung*, July 3, 2023, 9
2. *Berliner Zeitung*, July 4, 2023, 12

Cameroon was one of them from 1884 to 1919. Most of the Cameroon objects (41,000 of them!) were stored in Germany without being listed in museum directories.

When I returned home from our trip to Berlin, I saw an article in *The Christian Science Monitor Weekly* which spoke about "the genocide carried out by Germans between 1904 and 1908, when they controlled the colony of South West Africa," which is now Namibia.[3] For more about the Namibian tragedy, you might want to watch *Der Vermessene Mensch* (*Measures of Men*), a 2023 German film.

Once a great injustice is done, there is no way to get around it. One must deal with it openly, or have to live with it shamefully. The controversial Humboldt Forum building and museum complex opened in Berlin near Museum Island in 2020. It is supposed to deal with such issues, but it was unclear to me in 2023 whether this institution would be up to the task.

Nonetheless, it seems many Germans (especially Berliners) are very contrite about unfortunate things that happened in the past and want to make corrections where that can be done. However, there should be limits to everything, even blame:

Blame & Shame

Forgiveness may be forever
    & maybe some of our anger,
but they're not anchored together,
    the former word to the other.

If we're honest, also candid,
    those forgiven may still be sad;
it makes no matter what's been said;
    those who forgive may still be mad.

---

3. *The Christian Science Monitor Weekly*, Oct. 23, 2023, 14

Even if you feel no sense of blame,
you may still have a sense of shame.

Martin Walser, a German novelist and playwright died on July 28, 2023, while we were in Berlin. In 1998, on being awarded the Peace Prize of the German Book Trade, he said of the Holocaust: ". . . if the media presents this past every day, I feel in myself something that begins to resist the permanent presentation of our shame."[4]

4. *German History in Documents and Images*, Volume 10. Writer Martin Walser Reflects on the Difficulties of Living with German Guilt, October 11, 1998

14

What Is *Gemütlichkeit?*

Now, SOME 60 YEARS after I began to speak German, I think I know what *Gemütlichkeit* means, at least to me. It is something I should have learned from my grandmother, who displayed so much *Gemütlichkeit*. It was Minno, not my parents, who usually went to church. And I think she insisted all her grandchildren attend Sunday school. For her, it was always *Gemütlichkeit* and never *Terroristador*. As a result, I have written the following poem.

Gemütlichkeit

Gemütlichkeit is peace of mind,
    peace of mind, peace of mind;
it blooms only in Soul-bent light,
    in Soul-bent light.

The gap between our peace of mind
    & what I call *terror-ist-a-dor*
has brought me back to see Berlin
    a city renewed & blind no more.

A *terroristador* knows no peace,
    Gemütlichkeit feels no terror;
they will never conclude a truce;
    the two do not fit together.

Let's not revive the old Berlin,
    not as Hitler or as nation;
we can learn lessons from the past,
    & retrieve all we think we've lost.

Peace of mind, peace of mind;
    nothing like peace of mind!

It has been a long journey from Oklahoma to Berlin and back again, from my student trip to my final one in 2023. On July 27, I saw an article in *The New York Times* that said "Translation apps could make learning foreign languages obsolete." [1] That reminds me how this whole story got started, when I was but a teen who thought the German language would be so easy to learn. How I struggled with it, and then doubled down by learning French. This and a little Spanish seem to frame much of my life. As a result, I have written the following poem:

Translating Ourselves

When we start translating ourselves
    from one language to the other,
we'll all be living witnesses
    that spirit is our true nature.

Every language is discrete,
    each offers something one can reach;
not one of them is obsolete;
    all have something we ought to teach.

1. *The New York Times*, July 27, 2023, 13

15

Berliner Luft

BERLINER ZEITUNG OF JUNE 27, 2023, informed me that the American Orville Wright brought his experimental plane to Berlin in 1909 and flew it at Tempelhof for nineteen minutes— nineteen minutes in *Berliner Luft* (Berlin air). This to the delight of thousands of Berlin spectators. In coming years, officials say, Tempelhof will continue to be a place of experimentation, a new urban center for art, culture, and creative industries. But for me, Tempelhof will always be somewhere *up in the air,* somewhere between late childhood and early adulthood.

In 1967, while I was working at Tempelhof, Los Angeles Mayor Sam Yorty and Berlin Mayor Heinrich Albertz signed an agreement that the two metropolises would become sister cities, in part because many actors, editors, and directors had worked both in Hollywood and Berlin.

There was a celebration of this at the 1967 Berlin Film Festival and also in Los Angeles. In the latter, all attendees were given little cans of *Berliner Luft.* I'm going to finish this book with a photo of a can of *Berliner Luft,* which I purchased from eBay one month after I returned from Berlin. I don't think these two-inch cans are produced anymore. I paid $7.99 for this small and whimsical tin can—this old can of *nothing but air*—plus $4.77 for shipping and tax. Was I ripped off? Maybe.

The label says this is the *"Original Berliner Luft mit dem besonderen Duft"* (with that special smell). Here, the term *original* doesn't mean "the first," but "from the actual source," that is *from Berlin itself!* I can imagine similar cans of *nothing but air* flying off shelves as purchased souvenirs soon after the Berlin Airlift and for many years later.

But when I read the words *"mit dem besonderen Duft"* on the label of the can, I realize those words are also part of the city's unofficial anthem, *"Berliner Luft."* Now, I've begun to wonder: Were some of these cans produced and sold because of this anthem and others because of the Airlift? Could it have been both? Sometimes there is truth in a metaphor.

I don't want to smell or even open this vintage can. I'll just keep it as a souvenir or memento of the Air Bridge between Berlin and me—*and you, too, dear reader.* It helps us remember we always have a choice between *Gemütlichkeit* OR *Terroristador!*